D1547510

Terrorists and Freedom Fighters

What is terrorism? Is the difference between terrorists and freedom fighters merely a matter of whose side you are on? Can the end justify the means? Terrorists protest in the same manner, but their motives may be national, political, religious, or cultural. The threat to the freedom of the man in the street is real and widespread. Should terrorism be controlled by the use of authorized violence and the death penalty?

In this book David Hayes outlines the background to the development of terrorism in different troublespots in the world today. He also discusses terrorism in the future and the danger of world-wide conflict being sparked off by terrorist activity.

DAVID HAYES was awarded a first-class degree in politics by the University of York where he has taught in the Politics Department for several years. He is the author of *Human Rights* in this series, and co-author of *Stalin* in the Wayland History Makers series.

People, Politics and Powers

Terrorists and Freedom Fighters

DAVID HAYES

For Sevim
 more than ever

First published in 1980 by
Wayland Publishers Limited
49 Lansdowne Place, Hove
East Sussex, BN3 1HF, England

Second impression 1982

Copyright © 1980 Wayland Publishers Limited

ISBN 0 85340 652 9

Phototypeset by Trident Graphics Limited, Reigate, Surrey
Printed and bound in Great Britain
at The Pitman Press, Bath

CONTENTS

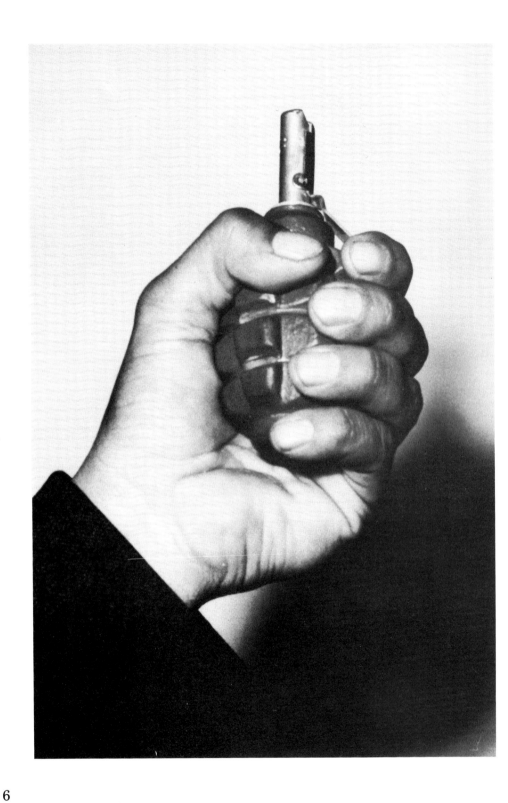

1 Introduction: Terrorism in the Modern World

On 30th May 1972 three students from Japan walked off an Air France jet at Lod Airport in Israel. In the airport terminal they collected their bags and pulled out the contents – hand grenades and VZT-58 assault rifles made in Czechoslovakia, provided by comrades in Italy. They then began calmly firing into the crowd.

In the carnage that followed twenty-six people were killed and eighty wounded. Most of those who died were pilgrims from Puerto Rico. Two of the terrorists also died – one shot himself, and the other was blown up by a grenade after slipping on the bloody floor. The third student, Kozo Okamoto, was captured when he ran out of ammunition.

The seeds of this incident were sown over two years earlier, in March 1970, when an internal Japanese flight was hijacked and diverted to Pyongyang in North Korea. The nine hijackers, who included Okamoto's elder brother, were members of a group called the Red Army. At their base in North Korea they came into contact with George Habash, leader of the Popular Front for the Liberation of Palestine (P.F.L.P.). Members of the Red Army travelled to P.F.L.P. training camps in Lebanon.

In January 1972 a new terrorist group was formed in Japan – the United Red Army. The P.F.L.P. recruited three of its members to carry out the Lod operation. Everything was carefully planned: forged passports, money, hotel bookings, airline tickets. After the massacre Ghaman Kanafani, a spokesman for the P.F.L.P., said that their purpose had been simply 'to kill as many people as possible'.

The Lod affair is just one example of terrorist activity. In the 1970s there has been a dramatic increase in terrorism throughout the world. Bomb attacks,

Opposite Hand-grenade of the type used in the Lod Airport terrorist attack.

kidnappings, assassinations, and armed robberies have become an everyday reality. What can be learned from the events at Lod about terrorism today?

First, terrorism is international. The terrorists at Lod were Japanese. The victims were mostly Puerto Rican. The setting was Israel. The weapons were Czech. The cause was Palestinian. And the impact was world-wide.

Secondly, terrorists always act for a purpose. The P.F.L.P. are fighting to create a homeland for the Palestinian people. They believed that this aim could be advanced by murdering defenceless travellers. This brutal project, however pointless it may seem, was designed to achieve certain goals.

Thirdly, terrorism is part of a cycle of suffering, destruction and hatred. Terrorism is both a response to, and a cause of, these circumstances. This cycle is

The bloody aftermath of the Lod Airport attack in which twenty-six people were killed.

Kozo Okamoto – sole
surviving terrorist of
the Lod Airport attack
– on trial.

continuous – one month after the Lod massacre,
Kanafani and his 17-year-old niece were blown to
pieces by a car-bomb, probably Israeli, in Beirut, Lebanon.

Fourthly, anyone can become the victim of terrorism. The victims at Lod were common people, as
'ordinary' as those who read about their fate. George
Habash has said that 'in today's world, no one is inno-
cent and no one is neutral'.

2 What is Terrorism?

The terms 'terrorism' and 'terrorist' arose from the events of the French Revolution of 1789. Following the overthrow of the monarchy, a group called the Jacobins took power and conducted a 'reign of terror' in France. The philosopher, Edmund Burke, wrote of 'thousands of hellhounds called terrorists' being 'let loose upon the people'.

The Jacobins inspired terror among the citizens by wielding state power. In the nineteenth century, however, the description of states and governments as 'terrorist' became less common. Instead the word came to denote revolutionaries who used violent methods against the state.

Terrorism is organized violence by small groups against the state for political purposes. There are four aspects to this definition. First, terrorist activities are organized, and involve conscious planning and direction. A kidnap or hijack attempt, for example, requires co-operation within an organized group. Secondly, terrorist projects are undertaken by small, usually secret bodies of armed men and women. Terrorist violence is not often undertaken by large groups of people, but by small groups excluded from power. Thirdly, terrorism – even when its victims are ordinary citizens – is directed against the state and its representatives. Fourthly, terrorism is used to further political aims. Terrorists are not just criminals. They may engage in armed robbery, for example, but this is part of a political strategy and is not done purely for material gain.

Terrorism is part of the modern political world. Terrorist groups consist of real people involved in real conflicts. The first task is not to condemn, but to understand them. One way of doing this is to ask: who are the terrorists?

10

Left Yasser Arafat (right) in consultation with fellow leaders of the P.L.O.

Below Women play an active part in terrorist activities – these women are members of the P.L.O.

The event which launched the French Revolution: the storming of the Bastille on 14th July 1789.

13

3 Who are the Terrorists?

In 1975 a conference of leaders from oil-producing countries in Vienna was besieged by a group of terrorists from various countries. Their leader was a 26-year-old Venezuelan, Ilich Ramirez Sanchez, alias 'Carlos' or 'the Jackal'. The son of a millionaire lawyer, educated in Cuba and the Soviet Union, trained in Palestine camps in Lebanon, active in operations in London and Paris – his background characterizes the new 'trans-national' terrorism. His youth is a typical characteristic of modern terrorists. Members of terrorist groups such as the Irish Republican Army (I.R.A.) and the Palestine Liberation

Hostages are driven through Vienna after terrorists had besieged a conference of oil ministers.

Organization (P.L.O.) may even 'graduate' through armed youth sections which provide education and training in the use of weapons.

Another characteristic is the large proportion of educated people involved in terrorist movements – especially among the leadership. A leader of the P.F.L.P., George Habash, was a medical doctor. Many members of the Baader-Meinhof Gang had been students. Their background is frequently middle-class. Andreas Baader's father was an academic, Gudrun Ensslin's father was a Protestant pastor, and Ulrike Meinhof's parents were art historians.

A third characteristic is the relatively large number of women terrorists. Twelve of the original twenty-two members of the Baader-Meinhof Gang were women. In 1977, 12 per cent of world-wide terrorist activity was carried out by women. In 1978, the figure had risen to 22.5 per cent.

Many terrorists have a religious background. Renato Curcio, founder of the Red Brigades in Italy, began his political career as a left-wing Catholic. So did Toni Negri, a professor of political science accused

The hostages are herded into a DC9 aircraft before being flown to Algeria at the terrorists' demands.

This young girl is trained in the use of weapons.

of involvement in Red Brigades' activity. Ernesto Cardenal, a member of the Sandinistas in Nicaragua, is a priest. In the 1960s another priest, Camillo Torres, joined the Army of National Liberation. He wrote that 'the Catholic who is not a revolutionary is living in mortal sin'.

Nationalist groups like the Basque E.T.A., the P.L.O. and the I.R.A. are more likely to attract members from the poorer classes, whereas groups emerging from student movements tend to have a largely middle-class membership.

Terrorist groups vary greatly in size. The Angry Brigade in Britain, the Symbionese Liberation Army in the U.S.A., and the Baader-Meinhof Gang in West Germany had less than twenty members each. The P.F.L.P. has about 3,500 members, while Al Fatah,

16

the biggest Palestinian terrorist group, claims to have 10–15,000 members. The Tupamaros in Uruguay had about fifty members in 1966, growing to 3,000 by 1971. Most groups operate in small units, thus making detection and capture more difficult. A major operation, like the Red Brigades' kidnap of Aldo Moro in 1977, involved the co-operation of about sixty terrorists.

Terrorists can be idealists or psychopaths, criminals or academics, peasants or urban workers. The varied membership of terrorist groups reflects the many different aspects of terrorism.

Andreas Baader – one of the founders of the Baader-Meinhof Gang.

4 Terrorism in the Past

Terrorism is not a new development. Violence by small groups against the state is as old as the state itself. In ancient times, religious sects like the Zealots fought against their Roman overlords. In the middle ages, mysterious religious groups called Assassins, founded in Persia, waged a long campaign against the empire of Saladin. In the sixteenth century, the Albanian fighter Skanderbeg resisted the armies of the Ottoman Empire for thirty years. Bandits called 'hajduks' maintained the tradition of opposition to Ottoman rule in the Balkan countries. Later, during the Napoleonic Wars, local fighters called 'guerrillas' harassed French invaders in Spain and Russia.

Local Russian peasant 'guerrillas' attack French stragglers during the Napoleonic Wars.

Tsar Alexander II of Russia.

Terrorism was first used as a weapon of revolution in the nineteenth century. In Russia, young student radicals – the 'populists' – believed that the assassination of the Tsar would spark off a popular uprising. In the 1870s they engaged in repeated attempts to incite the masses to revolt, but their efforts were met with savage reprisals. In 1881 a member of the 'People's Will' group finally managed to kill Tsar Alexander II. But the next Tsar ruthlessly suppressed the populists, and many fled to the West. Their example of 'propaganda by the deed' was taken up there – by the anarchists.

Between 1871 and 1914, bombings and assassinations were frequent weapons of struggle in France, Italy and Spain. Many terrorist actions of this period were the work of anarchists. Terrorist violence was also common in America, particularly during labour disputes. What did these terrorists hope to achieve? The Russian populists hoped to inspire the masses to revolt. In the West, however, the use of violence was more often an act of 'revenge' against the establishment. Some actions were simply a desperate protest against intolerable conditions.

Most terrorist groups in the past century have, however, had nationalist aims. In the 1860s, Irish Fenians fought for independence from British rule. Armenian terrorists, and the Inner Macedonian Revolutionary Organization (I.M.R.O.), worked

against the Ottoman Empire. The majority of terrorist groups between the two world wars were extreme
nationalists and anti-communists. The fanatical
I.M.R.O. and the Croatian Ustasha wanted freedom
from Yugoslavia. In a joint operation in 1934 they killed King Alexander of Yugoslavia. The Iron Guard in
Romania murdered two prime ministers in the 1930s
before coming to power in 1940. In the Middle East,
Zionist terrorists fought against British control of
Palestine.

There was little terrorist activity in Europe for a
long period after the Second World War. However, in
the 1950s and 1960s, the tradition of nationalist-
inspired terrorism continued elsewhere – in the 'third
world'.

The scene of the
explosion which killed
Tsar Alexander II.

21

5 The 1950s: Rural Warfare in Asia and Africa

The Second World War marked the end of the old imperialist network. A world dominated by two superpowers – the U.S.A. and the Soviet Union – was emerging. The defeat of Germany, Italy and Japan in the war meant the loss of their colonies. Britain and France could no longer ignore the claims of their subject nations for independence.

Nationalist movements in the 'third world' countries demanded political freedom and independence. Changes in the distribution of power were inevitable. In some countries, the transition to independence in the 1950s was relatively untroubled. In others, however, there was systematic violence.

The majority of the anti-colonial terrorists in the 1950s were rural-based. Industry was not widespread

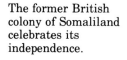

The former British colony of Somaliland celebrates its independence.

Above Chinese Red
Army soldiers struggle
through snow-covered
mountains during the
Chinese Civil War.

Left Rural settings
provide favourable
conditions for guerrilla
warfare.

Suspected Mau Mau terrorists are detained in a police cage.

in the 'third world' countries and most people lived on the land. The terrorists were given shelter, food supplies and popular support by many people in the rural areas. The city was the centre of colonial power. The terrorist strategy was to establish a firm base in the countryside from which they could attack the towns and cities. The example of Mao Tse Tung's victory in China in 1949, after a long war, was used to justify this strategy. His communist guerrillas had drawn support from the peasant masses, controlling first the countryside, then the towns.

The French fought a long and bloody war with the National Liberation Front in Algeria. In south-east Asia, France defended her interests against guerrillas in Vietnam before withdrawing in 1954. Britain held Malaya until 1957, countering the uprisings of local communists.

Britain, the major imperial power, was the main target of the post-war guerrillas. A series of battles was fought in Kenya, Aden, and Cyprus. In all cases, the military conflicts eventually led to British withdrawal. In Kenya in the early 1950s, a mysterious nationalist group called the 'Mau Mau' carried out a series of gruesome murders of white settlers in the remote highland areas, and of blacks who refused to help them. Many suspected Mau Mau supporters were killed or imprisoned. Among the latter was Jomo Kenyatta, who later became Kenya's first president. Kenyatta may have been involved in early Mau Mau activity, but it is unlikely that he masterminded it, as he was later accused of doing. The Mau Mau showed how a small, secret organization could make a dramatic impact with a campaign of selective terror.

In Cyprus, the terrorists of the National Organization of Cypriot Fighters, led by General Grivas, fought for 'enosis' – union with Greece – between 1955 and 1959. In Aden, from 1964 to 1967, British forces defended a small but strategically important region against South Yemen terrorists. In both cases, however, the focus of conflict was in the urban areas.

The pattern of rural warfare continued in some places into the 1970s. But terrorism had become increasingly urban-based. In the 1960s the transition from rural to urban terrorism took place in Latin America.

Jomo Kenyatta is sworn in as Kenya's first president in 1963.

6 The 1960s: Rural Warfare in Latin America

The word 'guerrilla' simply means 'little war' in Spanish. It was first used to describe the efforts of popular fighters who resisted the Napoleonic invasion of Spain in 1808. Later, the term came to be used with special reference to Latin America.

Rural guerrilla battles were fought throughout the sub-continent in the 1960s. Its nations had achieved independence from Spain and Portugal in the nineteenth century. They later became dominated by the economies of the U.S.A. and western Europe. The guerrillas wanted to sweep away this 'imperialism' together with its local agents – the army, landowners, and business magnates. The Cuban Revolution of 1959 was the first breach in this pattern of influence.

The victory of Fidel Castro and Ernesto 'Che' Guevara in Cuba had profound consequences in Latin America. The Cuban revolutionaries had marched to Havana, the capital, after conquering the country-side. Throughout the region, people felt that this victory would be only the first of a series. Many young revolutionaries believed that the tactics of guerrilla warfare – rural rather than urban terrorism – could be repeated elsewhere.

The emergent guerrilla bands thought that a few soldiers preaching 'liberation' to the peasantry could themselves create the conditions for revolution. But these 'years of effervescent heroism' were littered with defeats. In Cuba, the corrupt régime of President Batista had been widely detested. There was a vacuum of power at the centre. As a result, a disciplined commando group, such as that led by Fidel Castro, could triumph. But such conditions were absent in other countries, and the Cuban strategy was not appropriate. In Colombia, Peru, Argentina, Brazil,

Fidel Castro (right) and Che Guevara on their triumphant entry into Havana, capital of Cuba, in 1959.

and Bolivia the guerrillas suffered shattering blows from state forces.

In 1962, a guerrilla-provoked rising in Guatemala was crushed. In 1965 the guerrillas in Peru were defeated after a six-month struggle. Guevara had stated that 'it is the countryside that offers ideal conditions for the fight'. In 1967, he went to Bolivia to put his ideas into practice. After a struggle lasting under a year, 'Che' was killed and his guerrilla band was destroyed.

These defeats illustrate the weaknesses of the

Guevara (left) and
Castro discuss
strategy with
fellow guerrillas.

guerrilla movement. The relationship of the
guerrillas to the peasantry was an artificial one. Most
of the guerrillas came from the towns, and had little
knowledge of local conditions. They often met with
indifference or hostility from the common people.
Guerrilla leaders like Cesar Montes in Guatemala
and Fabricio Ojeda in Venezuela were also killed, but
it was Guevara's death alone that symbolized the end
of the rural strategy.

In fact the strategy of rural warfare did not com-
pletely die with Guevara. It persisted in Brazil until
1969, and in Colombia and Argentina into the 1970s.
But after suffering repeated military defeats, many
revolutionaries realized that a new approach was
needed. In the 1970s, the focus of the guerrilla movement in Latin America moved to the rapidly expand-
ing cities. Could this new strategy of the 'urban guerrilla' succeed?

7 The 1970s: A World-wide Problem

In the 1970s, terrorism moved to the centre of the world stage. The glare of publicity has made every terrorist action a 'media event', with all the qualities of a dramatic story – violence, suspense, emotion. The number of terrorist groups, and the frequency of their attacks, have increased. As communications between countries have become more sophisticated, so the

The kidnapped heiress, Patty Hearst, photographed during a Symbionese Liberation Army bank raid in 1974.

Members of the militant Black Panther Party marching in New York in the violent summer of 1968.

potential impact of the terrorist has become much more of a threat.

No country, however powerful, is free from the impact of political violence. The two 'superpowers', the U.S.A. and the U.S.S.R., have had to contend with terrorist attacks. In California, the Symbionese Liberation Army (S.L.A.) won intense publicity with its kidnap of the heiress, Patty Hearst. She later joined the group and took part in one of its raids. Like earlier U.S. groups – the Black Panthers and the Weathermen – the S.L.A. was smashed and its members killed or jailed. There have been cases of bomb attacks and arson in the U.S.S.R. In January 1979, three Armenians were executed for their part in the bomb explosion in the Moscow underground two years earlier which killed seven people.

The international character of modern terrorism can be seen in a number of ways. Terrorist groups may have their base in a 'neutral' country and often receive funds from abroad. A large number of terrorist actions are 'third country' operations. For example, in 1971 the Fighters for a Free Croatia killed the Yugoslav ambassador – in Sweden. In 1978, Armenian terrorists killed the wife of the Turkish ambassador – in Spain.

The more international a terrorist group becomes, the better are its chances of survival. The I.R.A. has been provided with funds and weapons by Colonel Gaddafi of Libya. The Palestinian cause had gained world-wide publicity by P.L.O. operations in many countries. The Soviet Union and China try to promote their 'progressive' image in parts of the 'third world' by supplying arms and money to guerrilla movements.

Conversely, a group without international links is vulnerable. The South Moluccan terrorists in Holland, for example, are waging a lone battle. They desire the independence of their islands from Indonesia, Holland's old colony, and have been campaigning since 1975, trying to force Holland to support their cause. But with only limited backing from the 40,000 Moluccans in Holland, and without external sources of support, the terrorists have little hope of success.

An Italian Communist has said that 'terrorism is like an infected boil, the symptom of a deeper disease ... a disease eating away the entire body'. This 'disease' has become a world-wide problem.

Black Panther Party members are forced to strip during a weapons check.

31

32

8 The Causes of Terrorism

The advanced industrial nations in western Europe, the U.S.A. and Japan, experienced a long period of economic growth after the end of the Second World War. Political stability accompanied this material prosperity. But the events of the late 1960s – student riots, workers' protests in many countries, and movements for 'black power' and against the Vietnam war – destroyed this stability. The world recession which followed the oil price rise of 1973 threatened the West's prosperity.

This union of economic and political crisis in the Western world encouraged the growth of extremist ideas. Various discontented groups – social, racial, national – harboured long-standing grievances against the 'affluent society'. Terrorist groups surfaced, quick to realize the value of publicity for their

Opposite Japanese students in conflict with riot police in 1969.

Left Paris, May 1968: students and workers proclaim 'unity and solidarity in the struggle'.

33

МЕЖДУ НАРОДИТЕ !

Angela Davis, a prominent black power leader, during a tour of the U.S.S.R.

cause. New technology and means of communication gave birth to a truly international form of terrorism.

This is the background to the growth of modern terrorism. But terrorist groups also arise from particular conditions, such as economic deprivation or social injustice. These grievances have been exploited by the I.R.A. and Palestinian terrorists. The Quebec terrorists have publicized the fact that standards of living in French Canada are often 40 per cent lower than those in the rest of Canada.

The more privileged sections of society have often produced terrorist groups. After the collapse of the student movement in the late 1960s, many embittered radicals turned to violence. In Japan, the U.R.A. developed from the Zengakauren group; the Students for a Democratic Society in the U.S.A. produced the Weathermen terrorists; terrorist groups created out of the ashes of student protest also emerged in Germany, Italy and Britain. In these cases, disillusioned people from the margins of society rejected the world their parents had made. This type of terrorism is more a hopeless and despairing reaction against the 'establishment' than a coherent attempt to change society.

Terrorism often begins as an alternative to a moderate and peaceful political strategy. As the older opposition groups gradually conform to society, younger and more extreme militants arise to replace them. For example, the Red Brigades began in opposition to the Italian Communist Party, which they believed had 'betrayed' the working classes. E.T.A.

Anti-Vietnam war demonstrations in Washington led to ugly clashes with military troops.

split from the conservative P.N.V., while the F.L.Q. broke away from the moderate Quebec nationalists. The new groups thought that the traditional groups were not determined enough to secure real change. Terrorism here arises from a feeling of betrayal, disappointment, or lost opportunity.

British women protest against the fighting in Vietnam.

Terrorism never simply happens; it can always be traced back to definite causes. Terrorist groups emerge in response to particular circumstances, and their aims and character differ accordingly. The next eight chapters examine the operations of individual terrorist groups in the modern world.

9 'Urban Guerrillas' in Latin America

Tupamaro chief –
leader of the notorious
Uruguayan terrorist
group.

After Che Guevara's death the focus of terrorism in Latin America shifted to the cities. The crowded urban areas were the source of great social tension, and offered terrorists both protection and support. The early 1970s were years of bitter violence as 'urban guerrilla' groups in Argentina, Uruguay and Brazil tried to provoke a revolutionary crisis.

The most successful of the urban terrorist groups was the Tupamaros in Uruguay. They staged spectacular bank raids and kidnappings, and broadcast propaganda after seizing local radio stations. In a daring raid in 1971, they engineered the escape of 108 of their members from prison, including their founder and leader, Raoul Sendic. At the same time, they released the British Ambassador to Uruguay, Geoffrey Jackson, whom they had seized eight months earlier.

The Tupamaros' success provoked the government and army into retaliation. In a small country of three and a half million people, an efficient military backlash could crush resistance. In the election of 1972, a 'broad front' of leftists – supported by the Tupamaros –

Geoffrey Jackson before and after his release by the Tupamaro guerrillas.

received only 18.3 per cent of the vote. The military intervened shortly after: rights were suspended and mass arrests took place. Sendic and his three fellow leaders were killed.

An urban terrorist campaign began in Brazil in 1968 with the formation of the Action for National Liberation by Carlos Marighella. The A.N.L. kidnapped many foreign diplomats, including the U.S. ambassador, winning the release of over one hundred political prisoners. In 1969, Marighella was killed in a shoot-out with police in Sao Paulo; his successor, Camara Ferreira, was also shot dead.

In Argentina urban terrorism began on a major scale in 1970 with operations by the People's Revolutionary Army (E.R.P.) and the Montoneros. The latter group kidnapped and murdered ex-President Aramburu. The E.R.P. was founded in 1969 as the military wing of the Revolutionary Workers' Party by Mario Roberto Santucho. Under his leadership, the E.R.P. gained a 'Robin Hood' image, kidnapping diplomats and businessmen, and releasing them only when food and clothing were given to the poor. The E.R.P. engaged in mass attacks on military garrisons. In 1974, they opened a rural front in the north-east province of Tucuman. In months of jungle fighting 600 E.R.P. militants died. On Christmas Eve 1975, an assault on a military arsenal in Buenos Aires cost a further 100 lives. In March 1976, an army take-over destroyed the last centres of resistance. In July, Santucho himself was killed, along with other E.R.P. leaders.

Despite severe repression, terrorists remain active in other countries under military rule. Sustained terrorist campaigns have been waged in Colombia, El Salvador and Nicaragua. In Nicaragua, the Sandinistas' most recent campaign against the dictatorship of General Somoza began in 1972. In August 1978, twenty-six terrorists seized the National Palace, holding MPs hostage in exchange for political prisoners. A civil war resulted in which thousands died and as a result of American pressure General Somoza was forced into exile. Two days later the Sandinistas were able to seize power. In Nicaragua, as elsewhere in Latin America, terrorism and military repression seem locked in a deadly embrace.

Opposite Sandinista guerrilla leader waves to his followers after releasing the hostages held in the National Palace.

40

41

10 Conflict in the Middle East

On 11th March 1978 two commando boats containing eleven Palestinian terrorists landed on the Israeli coast, midway between Tel Aviv and Haifa. Armed with grenades, explosives, and anti-tank missiles, they captured a bus full of weekend trippers, and drove fifty kilometres along the highway, shooting at passing cars. A police blockade stopped them, and in the shoot-out which followed they blew up the bus. Thirty-nine people were killed in the raid, many of them young children.

In swift retaliation, Israeli planes swooped on Palestinian bases in southern Lebanon. Many

Opposite Many Palestinians crossed the River Jordan and became refugees in neighbouring countries.

These new blocks of flats in Palestine are reserved for Jewish settlers.

Above German police attempt to capture the terrorists who hold the eleven athletes hostage at the Munich Olympics.

Right Hooded member of the 'Black September' group which was responsible for the murder of the athletes.

44

civilians as well as active terrorists were killed by the Israeli bombs. The Israeli Prime Minister, Menachim Begin, called the Palestine terrorists 'a gang of murderers' and 'the darkest force of reaction in the contemporary world'.

These incidents are part of the long campaign waged by the Palestinians against Israel. The roots of this campaign lie in the events following the Second World War. The creation of Israel in 1948 provided a permanent homeland for the Jews, six million of whom had been murdered by the Nazis during the war. But the founding of the new state in ancient Palestine involved the expulsion of three-quarters of a million Palestinians from their homeland. The Palestinians became refugees in nearby countries – Syria, Jordan, Lebanon. The Jewish people had found their homeland, but the Palestinians had lost theirs. This is the heart of the 'middle east problem'.

In the poverty of their refugee camps, Palestinian children learned of the fate of their people. Many grew up determined to fight to regain the lost territory. At first they relied on the Arab states, who were also hostile to Israel. But in 1967, Israel won a war

Beirut, capital of Lebanon, displays the contrast between wealth and poverty that is one element in the growth of terrorism.

President Sadat of Egypt, President Carter of the U.S.A., and Prime Minister Begin of Israel present their 'peace plan' for the Middle East.

against the Arabs in only six days. Israel occupied new territory in Gaza and the west bank of the River Jordan, bringing a further half million Palestinians under foreign rule. In this climate, Palestine militants intensified their terrorist campaign against Israel.

The terrorists are divided into several factions. Most belong to the Palestine Liberation Organization (P.L.O.), an 'umbrella' grouping with many agencies under its control. It wants to create an independent Palestine state on present Israeli territory. Within the P.L.O., the main terrorist arm is Al Fatah. Members of Al Fatah – the 'Black September' group – were responsible for the murder of eleven Israeli athletes at the Olympic Games in Munich in 1972. Al Fatah is the largest Palestinian terrorist group, but there are many others. The P.F.L.P., formed in 1967, is an extreme left-wing group which has been involved in some of the bloodiest operations of the war. They have taken the struggle beyond the middle east, co-operating with terrorists from Germany, Japan, and Turkey. Many foreign terrorists have trained in Palestinian camps in Jordan and Lebanon.

Violence and the middle east seem inseparable. A bloody war between Christians and Muslims in Lebanon in 1975–6 cost 60,000 lives. The treaty signed between Israel, Egypt and the U.S.A. in 1979 hopes to bring peace to the whole region, but the Palestinians reject this treaty and brand Sadat, the Egyptian leader, as a 'traitor'. The Israelis refuse to negotiate with, or even recognize, the Palestinian organizations. In an atmosphere of mutual hatred and mistrust, the prospects for an end to the conflict seem bleak.

Smiles all round as the leaders shake hands after signing the Peace Treaty.

11 Northern Ireland: the I.R.A.

For over ten years a bloody conflict has dominated life in Northern Ireland. In this small country of one and a half million people, 2,000 have been killed and thousands more injured. Terrorist groups from the Protestant and Catholic communities are fighting each other and the British Army. The victims include children and ordinary civilians as well as soldiers and policemen. Political violence has become a constant threat to life and property in Northern Ireland.

Such violence has ancient roots. In the Elizabethan age, Irish clans resisted the expansion of English colonizers beyond the 'pale' – the area around Dublin. In the late eighteenth century rival secret societies –

The Belfast riots of 1886: a Protestant crowd opposed to Gladstone's plan for 'home rule' for Ireland is charged by police.

48

Catholic 'Whiteboys' and Protestant 'Defenders' – fought over land and religious issues. Irish guerrilla forces were active in the 'war of independence' against British rule from 1919 to 1921.

The presence of the British Army has become a part of every day life for people in Northern Ireland.

This war won freedom for the twenty-six southern counties of Ireland. But the six counties of Northern Ireland – or 'Ulster' – remained within the U.K. The majority of the population there were Protestants. The remaining half million people were Catholics, and resented their inferior position in the new state.

The I.R.A. began as a movement to win independence for the whole of Ireland in 1916. Their campaigns in the 1930s and 1950s to bring Ulster into union with the rest of Ireland failed because of lack of support from the Catholics. In the 1970s, however, they renewed their campaign. A 'civil rights' movement arose among the Catholics in Northern Ireland in the late 1960s, as an attempt to achieve equality with their Protestant neighbours. Many Protestants reacted violently to its programme of marches and demonstrations. Street-battles escalated into open

The statue of Sir Winston Churchill looks on as smoke rises from Westminster Hall following an I.R.A. bomb attack.

warfare between sectarian mobs, with the Ulster police – the Royal Ulster Constabulary (R.U.C.) and the 'B-Specials' – backing the Protestants in an unequal struggle. In August 1969, after nearly a year of violence, the British Army was called in as a peace-keeping force.

The I.R.A. split into two factions in 1970. The 'Official' I.R.A. favoured political as well as military action, and had a Marxist outlook. The newer 'Provisional' I.R.A. was the larger group, more militaristic in its ideology, and was determined to fight both the Protestants and British forces. The 'Provos' waged a major campaign in the early 1970s, killing prison officers and policemen, civilians and soldiers.

In one incident in July 1972 nine bombs planted in Belfast's city centre killed eleven people and injured many others. Both I.R.A. factions have carried the war to England – a 'Provo' operation in Birmingham in 1974 killed twenty young people in city-centre pubs.

There was widespread condemnation of the I.R.A. bomb attacks on 27th August 1979 in which Earl Mountbatten lost his life, and seventeen soldiers were killed on the border.

An extreme breakaway group of sixty terrorists called the Irish National Liberation Army (I.N.L.A.), formed in 1974, has also been active in England. In April 1979 they killed Airey Neave, Conservative spokesman on Ulster, with a car bomb planted in the House of Commons' car park. In the same year the I.N.L.A. was declared an illegal organization by the British Government.

British soldiers survey the destruction following an attack on a bar in the docks area of Belfast.

Protestant terrorists have also caused many deaths – the Ulster Volunteer Force and the Ulster Freedom Fighters have murdered over 200 Catholics since 1972. The I.R.A. suffered great losses in 1976 and 1977, but in the following year they began to reorganize their forces into smaller and more efficient units. With safe havens in the Irish Republic, and supplies of weapons and money from sympathizers, Irish terrorists have the resources to prolong their struggles.

12 West Germany: the Baader-Meinhof Gang

The peace of a quiet autumn day in Cologne was shattered by a bloody ambush. The path of two cars, driving along a side-street, was blocked by an empty pram. At that signal, five gunmen emerged from a waiting van, spraying the cars with bullets. The driver and the three bodyguards were killed, and the man they were hired to protect was kidnapped.

It was 5th September 1977. The kidnap victim was Dr. Hanns-Martin Schleyer, head of the employers' federation in West Germany. For six tense weeks, fear of terrorism reached fever pitch throughout the country. While the government negotiated for Schleyer's release, a huge police hunt for his captors was staged.

The terrorist enemy was the Red Army Faction (R.A.F.), the remnant of an earlier group named after its founders, Andreas Baader and Ulrike Meinhof. The Baader-Meinhof Gang had grown out of the student movement in West Germany in the late 1960s. At first their terrorist activities were limited to arson and bank robberies. Then in 1972, they bombed U.S. military bases as a protest against the Vietnam war. Eventually most of their members suffered death, imprisonment or exile.

By 1977 the original terrorists were no longer active. Ulrike Meinhof killed herself in May 1976, while awaiting trial, and Holger Meins died on hunger strike in 1974. Over one hundred terrorists were in prison, and others were in hiding abroad. Only a small hard-core of activists – no more than fifty – were prepared to continue the fight against the state. In April, they killed Siegfried Buback, the Chief Public Prosecutor. In July, a leading banker, Jürgen Ponto, was shot dead in Frankfurt. The Schleyer kidnap was the latest incident in this wave of terror.

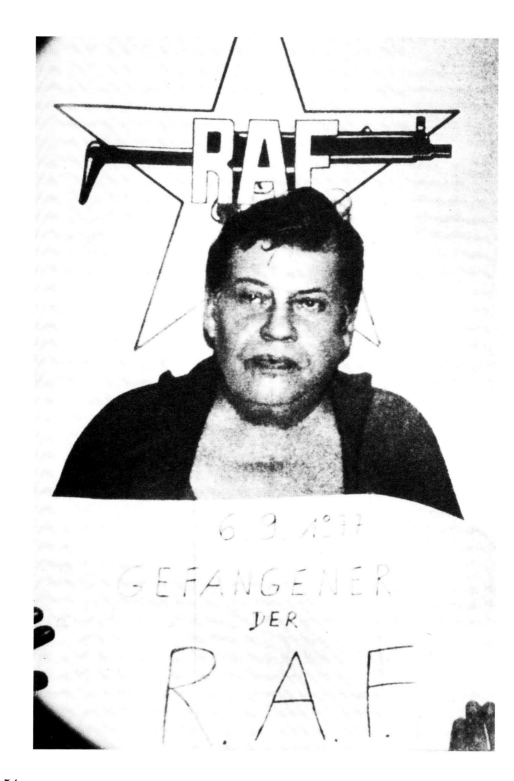

The kidnappers demanded the release of eleven of their comrades from prison, with payment to each of them of £25,000 and safe conduct to a country of their choice. The government played for time, and the terrorists grew impatient. The hijack of a German airliner was arranged. On 13th October, four Palestinians took command of a flight from Majorca to Frankfurt. They repeated the demands of their German comrades, adding a ransom of £9 million for the release of the eighty-four hostages on board and two Palestinians jailed in Turkey. The terrorists shot the captain of the plane, Jürgen Schumann, and the plane was flown by the co-pilot to Mogadishu in

Opposite The photograph of Hanns-Martin Schleyer released by his kidnappers.

Below The burial of Hanns-Martin Schleyer, attended by industrial and political leaders as well as relatives and friends.

Somalia, where Schumann's body was dumped on the runway. After an ordeal lasting four days, during which time the terrorists were preparing to blow up the plane unless the governments met their demands, the plane was stormed by German paratroopers. Three terrorists were killed, and the other was captured, and all the hostages were freed.

But the bloodshed was not over. On the 18th October the bodies of three terrorists – Andreas Baader, Gudrun Ensslin, and Jan-Carl Raspe – were found in their high-security prison cells. On hearing of the result of the hijack attempt, and the crushing of their hopes of freedom, they had committed suicide. The next day Schleyer's body was found in the boot of an abandoned car in Mulhouse, eastern France. After the events at Mogadishu, his kidnappers had finally shot him.

Members of the Baader-Meinhof Gang – Jan-Carl Raspe and Andreas Baader – who committed suicide in prison.

Ulrike Meinhof – the most wanted woman in Germany – after her arrest.

Police poster offering a one million mark reward for the arrest of German terrorists.

These events dealt a severe blow to the German terrorists. There was world-wide disgust at the murder of Schleyer and Schumann, and the German people renewed their support for the government in its fight against terrorism. In the following eight months, eleven terrorists were arrested. But despite the state's firm counter-measures, the deep-rooted fear of subversion persists.

13 Italy: the Red Brigades

The Italian people were stunned by the events of 16th March 1978 in Rome. On that day Aldo Moro, President of the ruling Christian Democratic party, was kidnapped with ruthless efficiency. At 9.15 a.m. the convoy of cars taking Moro to parliament was attacked. In the shoot-out that followed five of Moro's bodyguards were killed.

Moro was Italy's leading politician and had been Prime Minister five times. His captors were a group called the Red Brigades, which demanded the release of its jailed comrades including Renato Curcio, their leader. For two months the terrorists played a deadly game with the government, releasing letters from and photographs of their prisoner. Then, on 9th May, the police received a brief telephone call: 'In the Via Caetani there is a red car with the body of Moro'. Eleven bullets had been fired at close range into his body. The massive nationwide search for Aldo Moro was over.

The Red Brigades were forged out of the revolt of students and workers in Italy in the late 1960s. Their members were Marxists disgusted with the 'gradualist' policy of the Communist Party (P.C.I.). They believed in violence as a means of changing society. Their leader, Renato Curcio, declared at his trial that Moro's murder was 'an act of revolutionary justice. It was the highest act of humanity possible in this society divided into classes.'

The Red Brigades came to prominence in the mid-1970s. After the elections of 1976, the P.C.I. held the balance of power, but chose to support the government. This 'betrayal' angered the Red Brigades, and they increased their attacks on all members of the 'establishment'. They killed and wounded journalists, judges, businessmen and politicians. The victims of terrorism rose from fourteen in 1976 to over fifty the following year.

The Moro kidnap was intended to disrupt the trial in Turin of forty-nine people charged with terrorist offences. The trial had already been postponed twice because of Red Brigades' attacks and intimidation. The main accused (including Curcio) were housed in a special cage in the courtroom. Three hundred other

Italian students raise a flag to commemorate the 100th anniversary of the founding of the anarchist movement.

members of left-wing terrorist groups are still in jail, awaiting trial.

The terrorist network has not been broken. During the election campaign of May-June 1979, army units were brought in to help the three police forces in protecting lives and property. But the Red Brigades still carried out a daring raid in Rome, seizing the Christian Democratic headquarters, setting off time-bombs and killing a policeman. The Red Brigades are now the biggest and best-organized terrorist group in Italy. In their war against the Italian state, Red Brigades squads continue 'to attack . . . in order not to be annihilated'.

14 Spain: the Basque E.T.A.

In December 1973 a car bomb exploded in the centre of Madrid, instantly killing the Prime Minister, Admiral Carrero Blanco, and his chauffeur. This daring assassination was a dramatic challenge to the dictatorship of General Franco. Two years later, Franco himself died after a long illness, and a period of slow transition to democracy began. The first elections for 40 years were held in 1977. Workers and students

Basque terrorists during a clandestine press conference in which they claimed responsibility for the murder of Admiral Carrero Blanco.

began to organize themselves freely. Regional minorities in Galicia, Andalucia, and Catalonia demanded more control over their affairs. It was a group from one of Spain's national minorities – the Basque E.T.A. – which had planned and carried out Blanco's assassination.

'E.T.A.' stands for Euzkadi ta Azkatasuna (Basque Homeland and Freedom). The two and a half million Basques live in the northern provinces of Spain and the south-west provinces of France. They have a long history of opposition to the central government. Their culture and language differs from the rest of Spain, but under the Franco régime their language and national flag were banned. In response to this oppression, E.T.A. was formed in 1959 by students who were dissatisfied with the moderate policy of the Basque Nationalist Party (P.N.V.). The Basque Separatist movement demands the right to full independence from the rest of Spain. Their terrorist operations began when they organized bank robberies and the derailing of a train. Later they concentrated on the assassination of police and military figures, killing over sixty people in the first five months of 1979.

In areas of the Basque country where E.T.A. is strong, local businessmen pay the terrorists large sums of money each month to ensure they will not be the victims of terrorist attacks. Although E.T.A. has split several times over questions of strategy and ideology, its permanent activists have substantial popular support. In the elections of 1979, a pro-E.T.A. party won 170,000 votes – 15 per cent of the total Basque votes. Despite offers of some local control from the government, E.T.A. have stated that 'the most Madrid will offer will be less than we want'.

E.T.A. has links with other terrorist groups in Italy, including a leftist group called G.R.A.P.O. (First of October Anti-Fascist Revolutionary Group). However, E.T.A. has the advantage over other terrorist groups of strong support from the local Basque population. Although many Basques would be satisfied with self-government within a federal Spain, E.T.A. is determined to fight for complete independence. On 25th May 1979, they assassinated three senior army officers in Madrid. Two days later, a bomb killed eight people and injured forty others in a

Opposite The scene of the explosion which killed the Spanish Premier.

King Juan Carlos shovels earth into the grave of Premier Carrero Blanco.

café patronized by rightists. In June 1979 they gained publicity for their cause by bomb attacks on Spanish resorts visited by many foreign tourists. The terrorist offensive in Spain has been heightening and fascist groups who want a military coup d'état are also active. But the Basque issue is at the centre of the struggle. The fears of many were expressed by the leader of the P.N.V., Carlos Garaichoechea, when he said 'Euzkadi is beginning to smell like Ulster'.

15 Political Violence in Turkey

The Republic of Turkey was created in 1923 by Kemal Ataturk out of the ruins of the Ottoman Empire. Modern Turkey belongs to both east and west – ancient traditions and advanced ideas exist side by side. Many elements of old and new are visible in the terrorist violence which threatens to engulf the country.

Kemal Ataturk – founder of the modern Republic of Turkey.

Terrorism in Turkey began in the late 1960s with student demonstrations and attacks on U.S. military bases. A Turkish group, Revolutionary Youth, trained in Palestinian camps, and in 1971 killed the Israeli consul in Turkey. After severe military reprisals, the terrorists went underground, only to resurface with a vengeance in the late 1970s.

Old and new exist side by side in Turkey. The market in Ankara . . .

A government of social democrats led by Bulent Ecevit took office in January 1978. In its first eighteen months, over 1,500 people were killed in political violence. The majority of the victims were young students engaged in a civil war between leftist and rightist factions. The leftists are split into many groups with competing ideologies, but they share hatred of 'fascism' and the influence of U.S. 'imperialism'. The rightists are more united – most belong to the youth section of the Nationalist Action Party (N.A.P.).

These factions are locked in an endless spiral of violence. In the urban areas of Istanbul and Ankara, rightist students attack coffee-shops frequented by their leftist enemies. After carefully selecting their victims, they shoot them on the spot. Leftist gunmen retaliate by attacking N.A.P. offices and meeting-places. Universities have been closed because of perpetual warfare on the campuses.

... and modern office blocks and flats towering above the city.

69

Bulent Ecevit during
his election campaign.

In some respects this pattern of terrorism continues a long tradition of rural violence. In rural Turkey, feuds between rival clans and families have been common for centuries. Many disputes are settled by the gun; revenge killings are then in turn necessary to preserve honour. Since 1950, the urban population of Turkey has grown from 3.6 million to 18 million. Vast numbers of young people have drifted to the cities to study or to search, often unsuccessfully, for work. Many are open to the appeals of political activists.

The violence does not only affect students. In February 1979, Turkey's leading journalist, Abdi Ipekci, was shot in Istanbul. In this climate of violence and instability, economic development is hindered and fears of a civil war or military take-over increase. The Prime Minister, Ecevit, has spoken of 'inhuman murders by those who wish to destroy the democratic régime'. Terrorist activity poses a very real threat to the survival of Turkey's fragile democracy.

16 Civil War in Zimbabwe/Rhodesia

Civil war has ravaged this wealthy country in southern Africa since 1972. The country has two faces, even two names. Its 200,000 white inhabitants call it 'Rhodesia'. The six million black inhabitants call it by its ancient African name, 'Zimbabwe'.

In May 1979, a coalition government of whites and moderate blacks was formed. Its leaders announced that a 'new era' of co-operation between the races had begun. But meanwhile, black guerrilla armies still control much of the countryside. Their forces are determined to overthrow the government and establish black majority rule.

Z.A.P.U. guerrillas in training in one of their many camps in Zambia.

Joshua Nkomo, leader of Z.A.P.U. leads his followers in singing and cheering.

In seven years of fighting, nearly 10,000 guerrillas have died. Their places have been quickly filled by a constant stream of recruits. The guerrilla fighters mount operations mainly in rural areas, but they have also penetrated into the heart of Salisbury, the capital city. In August 1977, an explosion in a shopping centre killed thirteen people and wounded seventy-nine others.

The guerrilla armies together form the 'Popular Front' movement. They are divided into two groups – Zimbabwe African People's Union (Z.A.P.U.) and the Zimbabwe African National Union (Z.A.N.U.). Both have bases outside the country. The forces of Z.A.P.U., led by Joshua Nkomo, are based in Zambia and Botswana. Nkomo's forces launch frequent raids into Zimbabwe/Rhodesia, where a further 2,000 Z.A.P.U. guerrillas are active. Z.A.P.U. receives weapons, including anti-aircraft missiles, from the Soviet Union. One of these was used to bring down an Air Rhodesia plane in February 1979, killing all fifty-nine people on board. In retaliation for such attacks, Rhodesian air strikes have resulted in the deaths of many Z.A.P.U. guerrillas.

The Z.A.N.U. army, led by Robert Mugabe, is based mainly in Mozambique. Z.A.N.U. claims to have 40–50,000 regular guerrillas, of whom 8,000 operate inside Rhodesia. In the past they received arms from China, but their weapons are less modern and sophisticated than Z.A.P.U.'s. Mugabe has claimed to have 'more recruits than guns'. This, however, has not prevented Z.A.N.U. forces from carrying out terrorist attacks.

The guerrillas have great support among the black population. The division within their ranks persists, however. This is partly due to personal rivalry between Nkomo and Mugabe. Tribal differences are also important. Nkomo's support comes from the Matabele people of the south-west of the country. Mugabe's power-base is among the Shona people who form two-thirds of the population.

Ian Smith, leader of Rhodesia's white community,

Robert Mugabe (left), leader of the Z.A.N.U. army, and Joshua Nkomo (right) at a press conference.

73

Opposite Bishop Abel
Muzorewa, the first
black prime minister
of Zimbabwe/Rhodesia.

declared the country's independence from Britain in
1965. In 1978 he masterminded an agreement with
the moderate black leaders, Muzorewa and Sithole.
Under this pact elections held in April 1979 allowed a
'one man, one vote' system for the first time. A new
government, headed by a bishop, Abel Muzorewa, was
formed. But the terrorists do not recognize this government, and claim that the election was a device to
keep the whites in real control.

The civil war, which began with attacks on isolated
white farms, has moved into the centre of Rhodesian
life. Ninety per cent of the country is under martial
law. In 1978 18,000 whites emigrated, and a third of
the country's 6,000 farms have been abandoned. The
terrorists are unlikely to give up their struggle for a
'free Zimbabwe' under black control.

Below Ian Smith
during the historic
speech in which he
declared Rhodesia's
independence.

17 Terrorist Aims and Ideology

There is no single philosophy to which terrorists adhere. The ideas of terrorists vary according to their particular circumstances. But on one principle they are united – they favour the use of violence.

The 'philosophy of violence' was first expressed in the nineteenth century. The anarchist leader, Bakunin, wrote that 'the urge to destroy is also a creative urge'. His companion, Nechaev, published a statement of principles called the 'Revolutionary Catechism', which declared that 'our task is terrible, total, universal and merciless destruction'.

The French philosopher, Jean-Paul Sartre, whose writings have influenced terrorist thinking.

In the twentieth century, the writers George Sorel and Frantz Fanon have argued that violent action undertaken by oppressed classes and peoples can in itself be a liberating force. The ideas of philosophers like Herbert Marcuse and Jean-Paul Sartre have also been influential in justifying the use of violence by the 'outcasts and outsiders' of society. 'The rebel's weapon', wrote Sartre, 'is proof of his humanity'.

Most terrorists, however, do not use violence for its own sake. A general defence of violence is not enough. They are aware of the need for a broader ideology, both to justify their actions, and to attract support. This may involve a rejection of the 'terrorist' label. I.R.A. and E.T.A. militants, for example, call themselves 'soldiers' in a 'war of national liberation'. The P.L.O. leader, Yasser Arafat, in his speech to the United Nations in 1974, said that 'whoever stands by a just cause . . . cannot possibly be called a terrorist'.

The aims of many terrorist groups are nationalist. Breton and Corsican terrorists in France, the Quebec Liberation Front in Canada, POLISARIO guerrillas in the Western Sahara – these groups are all fighting for the independence of their region. Terrorists fighting for national independence have certain advantages over other terrorist groups. A programme of 'national liberation' can be made to appeal to all social classes of the community. A nationalist programme may also contain a socialist appeal to workers and poorer people. Socialist ideas are favoured by terrorists because they attach importance to universal principles like freedom and equality. By focusing on general ideas and long-term goals, terrorists can play down short-term differences of opinion and clashes of interest among their supporters.

Many terrorists claim to be Marxists or Marxist-Leninists. However, Marx himself regarded terrorism as an immature and élitist method of struggle, a sign that social conditions were not yet ripe for revolution. When Irish Fenians bombed Clerkenwell Prison in 1867, killing 12 and injuring 120, he wrote of this 'very stupid exploit'. Lenin regarded terrorism as a tactic of minority intellectual groups – mass action, he believed, would make it 'unnecessary'. The opposition of most Marxists to terrorism has been for pragmatic and not moral reasons. In their view terrorism

Yasser Arafat, leader of the P.L.O.

is not immoral, but simply a negative and fruitless form of resistance.

Terrorist groups are not interested in developing a theory of terrorism. They believe that actions speak louder than words. Their attitude is typified by Ulrike Meinhof who said, 'A few dozen fighters, who go into action without endless talk, can fundamentally change the political scene.'

18 Terrorist Strategy and Tactics

In 1866 a Russian populist, Karakazov, attempted to assassinate Tsar Alexander II. After firing at the Tsar's passing carriage, he was arrested by citizens loyal to their monarch. As he was led away he shouted at them, 'Fools, I have done this for you!' This anecdote illustrates the pathetic aspect of terrorism. Almost all terrorists claim to act on behalf of 'the people', and their strategy is frequently designed to win support from the masses. Yet the result of terrorist action is often to unite the people in support of their government.

Modern urban terrorist groups deliberately try to provoke the state into brutal legal and military repression. Their thinking is that 'anti-terrorist' measures will reduce freedom and create resentment among the masses. The people will come to realize that the state exists only to oppress them, and they will finally rise up against the state, recognizing the terrorists as allies in a common struggle.

This 'strategy of provocation' has, however, failed repeatedly. In Uruguay a democratic régime was replaced by a military dictatorship as a result of the Tupamaros' campaign. The introduction of anti-terrorist laws in West Germany and Britain has not led to an increase in popular sympathy for the terrorists. The isolation of terrorists from the people, and their indifference to loss of life, has created hostility rather than public backing.

Terrorists use a variety of short-term tactics to advance their strategic aims. The kidnapping or assassination of leading figures – diplomats, military leaders, businessmen – is one of the oldest and most effective ways of attacking the state. In more recent times tactics like car bombs, letter bombs, and hijackings are being used. However, the use of traditional

Six aeroplanes are blown up by terrorists in Jordan in 1970.

methods can also reflect the belief that terrorists are fighting a traditional struggle with ancient roots. Basque militants fighting riot police in Pamplona have used the medieval tactic of pouring boiling olive oil from the windows of narrow streets. The climate of fear and disruption such attacks arouse is the terrorists'

strength. For small, relatively unknown groups like the South Moluccan and the Croat terrorists, train and aeroplane hijackings have been a means of achieving world-wide publicity.

Terrorists often choose tactics which achieve instant and visible success. The release of prisoners or the payment of a ransom can be a great propaganda boost as well as a practical victory. But such short-lived 'triumphs' can lead to the terrorists losing sight of their ultimate aims, and becoming concerned only to prolong their own existence. Terrorist violence, far from being a means of human 'liberation', becomes a futile cry of isolation and despair.

Right Letter bombs have proved a deadly weapon in the terrorists' armoury.

Below South Moluccan terrorists hold fifty-six passengers hostage on a hijacked train.

19 The State and Terrorist Violence

Governments have a responsibility to protect their citizens from violent attacks. They respond to the terrorist challenge in a number of ways. Many states have passed laws allowing police to detain suspected terrorists without trial. They have also set up special anti-terrorist commando squads, heightened security at public gatherings, and increased protection of prominent individuals.

Many terrorists have been tried and convicted. Long prison sentences – at least 15–20 years, sometimes life – have been passed on terrorists in Holland, Canada, Spain, West Germany, Britain, and Italy. In June 1978, the Japanese government introduced new measures, including the death penalty, for terrorist offences. The Israeli cabinet also voted in April 1979 in favour of executions of those convicted of 'inhuman terrorist crimes'.

Another way of dealing with terrorism is for the state to go over to the attack. In Nicaragua, President Somoza ordered the bombing of towns held by Sandinistas opposed to his régime, killing thousands of ordinary citizens as well as guerrillas. Rhodesian planes have raided guerrilla camps in Zambia and Mozambique, with heavy loss of life. Israeli air strikes against P.L.O. camps in Lebanon have caused many deaths. In the five months following the Black September raid during the Munich Olympics in 1972, Israel made 33 attacks on Palestinian camps in Syria and Lebanon, killing 1,000 people.

Terrorists often operate across national boundaries, but it is difficult for governments to do the same thing. An international court to try terrorists was first suggested after the assassination of King Alexander of Yugoslavia in 1934, but both the inter-war League of Nations and the United Nations have been

Trial of terrorists – are long prison sentences likely to deter terrorists?

unable or unwilling to take decisive action in this area. This has left states with the choice of breaking international law by acting alone. The Entebbe operation in the summer of 1976, when Israeli commandos freed hijack victims held by German and Palestinian terrorists in Uganda, took place without the consent of the Ugandan government.

Hijacking agreements, like the one made in 1973 between the U.S.A. and Cuba, have been successful. But uneasy or hostile relations between states hinder the fight against terrorism. Despite a treaty signed in 1975, West Germany and Yugoslavia have wrangled over the expulsion of refugee terrorists. In return for the murderers of Schleyer and Ponto, captured in Zagreb, Yugoslavia demanded that Croat terrorists living in Germany be returned – including their leader, Stjepan Bilandzic. Both sides are concerned to defeat 'their own' terrorists, showing little concern for the problems of other states.

The Prime Minister of Turkey, Bulent Ecevit, has

said that 'the improvement of social and economic conditions is essential before we can adequately deal with terrorism'. Similarly, the Dutch government in a report on the South Moluccan people in Holland, proposed improvements in their conditions – job subsidies, more language teachers, better housing – as a way of integrating the Moluccans into Dutch life, thus reducing the bitterness which can lead to acts of terrorism.

A member of the Tupamaro group who was sentenced to thirty years' imprisonment for multiple assassinations.

20 The Future of Terrorism

There is little evidence to suggest that terrorism will cease to be a problem in the future. Terrorism can be traced back to specific causes – national divisions, frustrated minority groups, racial and social tensions – and it seems likely that, far from decreasing, these tensions may well increase in the future.

Terrorism will continue to plague the world so long as it is an effective means of drawing public attention to a cause. The capacity to terrorize may well increase as more sophisticated weapons become available to terrorists. The provision of arms, money and shelter by pro-terrorist states will continue to be an invaluable support to terrorists. As news and pictures of terrorist attacks reach the mass of the population, the terrorist will become an increasingly powerful figure. However, the media does have an important role in ensuring that terrorism does not become an accepted fact of life. So long as the public is repulsed by the terrorists' callous indifference to loss of life, there is likely to be public support for government measures taken to combat terrorism.

The attitude of governments to terrorist attacks will be a determining factor in the continuing survival of terrorism. There is no easy solution to the dilemma of whether to give in to terrorists' demands in return for hostages, or whether individuals should be sacrificed in the hope that terrorism will cease to be an effective means of coercing governments.

What will be the attitude of future generations to terrorism? Today's terrorist can become tomorrow's hero. A leader of the Irgun Zvai Leumi, Menachim Begin, became Prime Minister of Israel. An ex-Chief of Staff of the I.R.A., Sean MacBride, was awarded the Nobel Peace Prize.

Leon Trotsky wrote that 'what distinguishes a

revolutionary is not so much his capacity to kill as his willingness to die.' The terrorists' readiness to die is perhaps their greatest strength. Kozo Okamoto made a full confession at his trial on condition that he be given a pistol to shoot himself (the promise was later broken). Abu Yusuf, the Chief of Intelligence of Al

Modern terrorist weapons – explosives, a timing device, and a detonator (hidden inside the toothpaste tube).

The modern face of terrorism – this tiny pistol may look like a toy but can in fact kill people.

Fatah killed by an Israeli bomb, had previously said, 'We plant the seeds, and the others will reap the harvest. Most probably we'll all die ... But the youth will replace us.' The 'defiant hopelessness' of the terrorists guarantees their survival.

In the late twentieth century terrorist actions will continue to have a dramatic impact. The number of people who have suffered from terrorist attacks is small in comparison with the victims of war, and the reaction evoked by the violence of terrorist groups may be out of proportion to the scale of their operations. But terrorism, like war, does not affect only its immediate victims: the terrorists' challenge to social peace and legal order is the concern of everyone.

Appendix

The major contemporary terrorist groups mentioned in the text are listed below in alphabetical order.

ACTION FOR NATIONAL LIBERATION Founded by Carlos Marighella in Brazil in 1968. Its leader was killed in 1969. Carlos Lamarca, leader of the breakaway ARMED REVOLUTIONARY VANGUARD, was killed in 1971.

AL FATAH *see* Palestine Liberation Organization.

ANGRY BRIGADE English group formed in the late 1960s with the help of Spanish FIRST OF MAY terrorist group. Its five leaders were convicted of conspiracy to cause explosions in 1972.

BAADER-MEINHOF GANG West German group, formed in 1970. Later known as the RED ARMY FACTION (R.A.F.) in imitation of the Japanese group of the same name.

CORSICAN NATIONAL LIBERATION FRONT Launched in May 1976 to win independence from France, it has been active in Corsica and on the mainland.

CROATIAN REVOLUTIONARY BROTHERHOOD Formed in Australia by Croatian exiles, it has been active in Sweden, Germany, Paraguay and the U.S.A.

ERITREAN LIBERATION FRONT Active against Ethiopia since 1961, with mainly Muslim support. The mainly Christian and more left-wing ERITREAN POPULAR LIBERATION FRONT split from it in 1970.

EUZKADI TA AZKATASUNA (E.T.A.) Basque group, formed in 1959, fighting for independence from Spain. It has now split into several factions.

IRISH REPUBLICAN ARMY (I.R.A.) Irish group, founded in 1916, active in the 1970s in Britain, Holland and Germany as well as both parts of Ireland. Split into the Provisionals and the left-wing Officials. The IRISH NATIONAL LIBERATION ARMY broke away from the latter in 1974.

MOVEMENT FOR NATIONAL LIBERATION (TUPAMAROS) Group in Uruguay, founded by Raoul Sendic in 1963, and smashed by a military coup in 1973.

PALESTINE LIBERATION ORGANIZATION (P.L.O.) Its main terrorist arm, AL FATAH, began operations against Israel in 1965. The smaller, more extreme POPULAR FRONT FOR THE LIBERATION OF PALESTINE (P.F.L.P.) was formed in 1967.

PEOPLE'S REVOLUTIONARY ARMY Founded in Argentina in 1969 as the military wing of the Revolutionary Workers' Party.

POLISARIO A guerrilla army fighting Morocco for the independence of the Western Sahara, trained and supplied by Algeria.

POPULAR FRONT *see* Palestine Liberation Organization.

QUEBEC LIBERATION FRONT (F.L.Q.) Founded in 1963 by George Schoeters. In 1970 they kidnapped a British trade commissioner and the Canadian Minister of Labour.

RED BRIGADES Italian group, emerged in 1969 with attacks in Milan and Genoa.

SANDINISTA FRONT OF NATIONAL LIBERATION Nicaraguan group, named after a general, Augusto Sandino, killed by U.S. marines in 1934. Their most recent campaign began in 1972, and they won power in 1979 after a civil war with the National Guard of President Somoza.

SOUTH-WEST AFRICAN PEOPLE'S ORGANIZATION (S.W.A.P.O.) Formed in 1957 and began operations in 1966. Fighting for the independence of Namibia from South Africa. A smaller group, the SOUTH-WEST AFRICAN NATIONAL UNION, has support only from the Herero people.

SYMBIONESE LIBERATION ARMY (S.L.A.)
American group of under a dozen people, mostly
white students and black prisoners, formed in 1973.
Its core was killed in a Los Angeles shoot-out in
May 1974.

ULSTER VOLUNTEER FORCE A 'loyalist' army
active in Northern Ireland since 1966 supported by
extreme Protestants. A breakaway group, the
ULSTER FREEDOM FIGHTERS, was formed in
1973.

UNITED RED ARMY Japanese group, formed in
1972, by fusion of two groups. Its forerunner, the
RED ARMY, had been active since 1969.

WEATHERMEN (later WEATHER UNDER-
GROUND) U.S. group, formed in Chicago in 1969.

ZIMBABWE AFRICAN PEOPLE'S UNION
(Z.A.P.U.) Formed by Joshua Nkomo in 1959,
banned the same year, with forces mainly based in
Zambia. Dissidents in the group formed the
ZIMBABWE AFRICAN NATIONAL UNION
(Z.A.N.U.) in 1963. The latter is led by Robert
Mugabe and is based in Mozambique.

Glossary

The following terms are defined according to their usage in the text.

ANARCHIST a person who engages in political activity in order to bring about a society which has no government or central authority.

ASSASSINATION the violent and illegal killing of an important person – for example, a politician, diplomat, monarch, military or religious leader.

COLONIALISM a system where one country has political control over dependent nations or 'colonies'.

DICTATORSHIP a political system where one leader or select group has complete control of the people.

FASCISM a system of government (often ruled by a dictator) which controls everything within a country and suppresses all public criticism. Such a system may be justified by extreme nationalist or racialist ideologies.

GUERRILLA a member of a small band of fighting men based in rural areas.

GUERRILLA WARFARE type of warfare conducted by guerrillas which depends on hit-and-run methods and avoids pitched battles with regular armies.

HIJACK to seize a vehicle (train, bus, aeroplane), often holding the passengers hostage in return for ransom money, publicity or political favours.

IMPERIALISM the exploitation of an undeveloped country by states or countries with strong economies.

MARTIAL LAW a period (usually during a war or national emergency) when a country is controlled by military forces and civil liberties may be temporarily suspended.

MARXISM the theory and practice of revolution brought about by the working classes, based on the writings of Karl Marx (German philosopher 1818–83).

NATIONALIST a person who fervently defends the independence and freedom of his country from the influence or domination of another nation.

PROPAGANDA political writings (pamphlets, manifestos, posters, etc.) issued by a state or group informing the public of their opinions with the aim of winning popular support.

REFUGEE a person who is forced to leave his country and seek refuge in another country.

REPRISAL a revenge attack on the enemy.

SOCIALISM a theory proposing a society without classes; in practice, an economic system based on control of the means of production and distribution by the state.

TAKE-OVER the seizure of the government of a state by a minority group.

Book List

a) General Works

Y. Alexander, ed., *International Terrorism*, Praeger, 1976

J. Bowyer Bell, *A Time of Terror*, Basic Books, 1978

R. Clutterbuck, *Kidnap and Ransom*, Faber, 1978

R. Clutterbuck, *Living with Terrorism*, Faber, 1978

C. Dobson & R. Payne, *The Carlos Complex*, Coronet, 1978

W. Laqueur, *Terrorism*, Abacus, 1978

G. McKnight, *The Mind of the Terrorist*, Michael Joseph, 1974

b) Case Studies

J. Becker, *Hitler's Children – the Story of the Baader-Meinhof Gang*, Panther, 1978

J. Bowyer Bell, *The Secret Army*, Blond, 1970

G. Carr, *The Angry Brigade*, Gollancz, 1975

C. Dobson, *Black September,* Macmillan, 1974

G. Jackson, *People's Prison*, Faber, 1973

A. Labrousse, *The Tupamaros*, Penguin, 1972

Index

Picture Acknowledgements

Associated Press, 39 (left), 64, 65, 66; John Griffiths, 27, 28; Keystone Press Agency, 6, 8, 9, 17, 29, 33, 44, (both), 46, 47, 54, 55, 56, 57, 58, 60, 61, 62, 70, 73, 82 (bottom), 84; Mansell Collection, 20–21; Popperfoto, 14, 15, 30, 34, 35, 36–7, 38, 39 (right), 41, 50, 63, 74, 75, 76, 80–81, 82 (top), 85, 87, 88; Turkish Tourism Information Office, 67, 68, 69; Ulster Museum, 49, 51, 52 (both); United Nations, 22; Z.A.P.U., 71, 72. All other pictures are from the Wayland Picture Library.